Transformation Messages Go FM Frequency
Getting Sales Without Struggle

by
Donna DeVane
The Barefoot Guru

Transformation Messages Go FM Frequency
Getting Sales Without Struggle

©Copyright 2013 Donna DeVane The Barefoot Guru
All rights reserved. Printed in the USA. No part of this book may be used or reproduced in any manner whatsoever without written permission except in the cast of brief equations for article reviews, audio or video or educational purposes.

For interviews contact the author at
donnadevane @gmail.com

Transformation Messages Go FM Frequency
Getting Sales Without Struggle

Sharing your passions for success

by Donna DeVane The Barefoot Guru

Other print Books by Donna DeVane

A Journey Back To Self
How to Thrive in a Survival Mindset World
How to Stay Motivated For Success

Plus several Kindle books available at Amazon
and AwakenedRadio.net

Acknowledgments

Big hug and Thank You to my family, friends, radio listeners, YouTube watchers, and readers. You have all inspired me to follow my passion and live an adventure.

Thank you also to everyone who has discourage me. You allowed me to reach down deep inside to find courage, power and to Remember Who I Am.

Contents

Introduction..6

Chapter One...8
   Frequency Overview
   Ham Radio Broadcasting

Chapter Two...18
AM Frequency

Chapter Three...24
FM Frequency

Chapter Four...29
Getting the Message Out

Chapter Five..37
Sharing YOU

Chapter Six..47
No More Puff n Fluff

Chapter Seven...61
Pulling it all Together

Thank You...64

Introduction

There is a new energy going around. Some are calling it The Shift, or Transformation; it makes no difference what it's called because it's happening. People all around the world are feeling something that perhaps they can't put into words, but they are feeling it nonetheless.

That's what this book is all about. That feeling, that energy, whether it's felt subtly or with a bang. As a coach, author, teacher or radio broadcaster you are aware of it too. That's why you've written the book, prepared the call or host your radio show. It's why you do what you do. You feel the call to share your wisdom with others in a real and meaningful way.

Now you are wondering just how to get the word out to those who are ready for it. This is where this books comes in.

I will take you through the steps of Sharing Not Selling. When you have applied these principles you will connect with just the "right" people to get your word out. It's not about hype.. it's about being REAL.
As a teacher, author, life coach and even talk radio host, I've heard from people who are really tired of the old way of hard sales. It consumes you, wears you out and leaves little time for working on your next inspired project or just simply living your life.
When I started Awakened Radio Network I had no idea of how to do it, I just knew I had to. There were plenty of people telling me why I couldn't and even a few who encouraged me to go ahead with the dream. I am grateful to both sides of the story, as they equally provided me with opportunities to look more deeply within myself for answers.

This book is all about what I've discovered along the journey of getting the word out about the radio station, Thrive Evolutionary Consciousness Magazine and my own books and coaching programs.

I encourage you to go through this book like a meditation, allowing your own answers to come to your awareness as you read and do the exercises. Keep a notebook handy to write down all those AHA moments.

For those who would like to work one on one with me please visit AwakenedRadio.net & check out the Divine Connections section of the store. You will see the FM Frequency course there.

Chapter One
 Frequency Overview
 Ham Radio Broadcasting

Since I'm station owner of Awakened Radio I think in terms of broadcasting and how to connect with people all over the world so they can hear the messages of our hosts. Also I enjoy explaining things using examples, it's how I think. Pictures appear in the movie screen in my head and I say them or write them down. It makes it easier and simpler to get my point across.

This is a part of what this book is about. How to really connect with the people who are asking for your book, coaching, classes or radio broadcast. How do you really connect with the people who are already asking for what you are offering?

You have made many twists and turns on the journey that brought you to your present experience of yourself. You've had millions of AHA moments. They've become the foundation of your book, class, etc. What you KNOW is what you are reaching out to share with others.

Let's say that your project is prime. You know the information works because you worked it in your own life. Now you are at the point of sharing the process, insights, principles with others so that they too can expand their conscious creating.

You've done all the stuff you are supposed to do. You've blogged, created a website with a newsletter, you've given FREE STUFF out the yang yang. You've done webinar after webinar and while people show up to get the FREE STUFF not much else happens. You send out a weekly newsletter pitching your product over and over again with the result that most of the emails don't get opened or people just unsubscribe.

What's Going ON Here???? You ask that over and over. You have read the books on marketing, perhaps you've even taken a few classes on it. Let's look at this and find the energy of it. Energy is everything. Everything is energy. This is what matters. Thoughts, actions, beliefs, words; it's all energy.

Back years ago I was looking for information on how to get more sales of my products on my website. I bought several books & even listened to a few audio books by the "famous method teachers". One thing really stood out for me. They all sounded like used car salesmen or those guys at the fair shouting at you to give them a dollar for three tosses of a ball that would surely result in you winning the giant teddy bear.

I knew that it just didn't "feel right" to me. There was something about the energy of these hard sales pitches that almost made me itch. Now these were "spiritual teachers" sharing this information & it didn't feel very spiritual to me. It felt old, itchy, scratchy & uncomfortable. Something about it just didn't set right with me on an energy level. It wasn't just that so many of the books were little more than sales pitches to buy their other books either, although that was a part of it.

The overall method, the principles of "selling" just didn't fit with what I was selling. I began looking at the people who were buying these other people's classes and books. They all had a feeling of desperation, chaos & a churning energy about them. What I was selling didn't feel like that. I was offering principles to experience insightful, intuitive, empowered life with.

There just wasn't a match of the energy. No wonder I felt odd about the methods of selling. I wasn't selling a method... I was sharing wisdom. I was offering my own journey, my insights, how I had traveled as a guide for those who were at the same place I had been in before the book or class was created.

Selling just wasn't what I was doing. I was sharing.

Now let me get back to the frequencies part. There are three main frequencies that I want to talk about. The first one is "ham radio". Understand there is nothing wrong with this manner of communication. It's been around for a very long time and has served us well before we had other technologies. A lot of people still use it to talk with people around the globe.

For this book and explanation however, I will use it as the example for those who are broadcasting, whether in a book, radio show, class, coaching or course in order to share their fear, frustration and anger with others.
I'm talking about energy of the message and energy of the sharing here, not a review on the type of broadcasting or broadcaster. All messages have listeners. We are all at different places in our experience of consciousness and it's all equally good. I'm only pointing out that working with the same energy, bandwidth or frequency for the whole project is where the easiest success lies.

Let's look at the message of the "ham radio frequency". Running Awakened Radio has helped me to understand a lot of things about people. I am surprised by how many come to the station looking to get on the air & feel that their message of fear, anger & chaos is what we are all about. They consider themselves to be Awake to what's going on.

In truth they are awake to the energy of fear that has created all the experiences they want to talk about. The chaos we have all co created is the result of our fear, stress and anxiety. We are the ones with the power bringing about the experiences we are all watching unfold and playing with.

Awakened Radio is not about the FEAR, it's about how we create with it and how by changing the energy we create with we then change the creation. I get that, most of the people who come to the station get that, but a few don't. It's ok that they don't. There are plenty of stations for the Ham Radio broadcaster. I am helpful and show them the way.

In the beginning of learning how to run a station I let a few Ham Radio broadcasters on the air. They didn't stay long. Why? It's the energy again. The energy of the station is FM not Ham. It feels different to everyone, even if people don't understand what they feel, they still feel it and are affected by it.

Needless to say these broadcasters don't stay around long. Their listeners just don't show up. People don't listen to their archives. Why is this? Simply put, their frequencies don't match the frequencies of the station overall. The station is FM, their broadcast is Ham. It doesn't fit. The same thing would happen if I took my broadcast "Healing Circle" over to a conservative Christian station.

There is no fit of energy, no compliment, no foundation upon which to build. It's like mixing up your building materials and hoping to create a house of brick. If you don't use brick you don't get a brick house, you get a mixture of all the materials used.

The same is true with YOUR message. The energy of the message always expands, that's the creative principle. Whatever is set in motion always seeks to experience more of itself. When put in terms of how to "sale" your message think of it this way. You have a sure fire way that works for people to move out of fear, stress & anxiety. You have used this wisdom yourself & know it works and share in your book the process of moving from fear into wisdom.

Where would you share this information? Would you go to a fear based platform or look for and interact with a platform where the energy matched or was higher than the energy of your book? Of course you would take the second option.

But.. and it's a BIG But.. if you are still trying to sale with webinars based on sales pitches, with the energy of hurry, hurry, the deal ends in 24 hours and such you have gone to the fear based platform. I've had many people come to me over the time Awakened Radio has been on air and share with me how I need to put pop ups all over the place getting people's email addresses so that I can market to them!!!

WHAT?????

Here is why I don't do that. Awakened Radio is a people supported radio station. We don't do the corporate sponsored advertising every few minutes energy. I built it that way on

purpose. Awakened Radio is about all of us understanding the energy and co creating a place for our messages.

At one point I listened to a few people and incorporated their ideas. I began feeling a headache whenever I went to the website. I realized that the energy of the website and the station were out of whack. It didn't feel good. My chakras were taking in all the contrast and busy busy of the station website while listening to a message that wasn't built on the busy busy hurry hurry energy.

I immediately revamped the website. I brought it back into alignment with the energy of the station overall and at once began hearing from people how much better they liked it. Now realize that before the changes it was colorful, bright, shiny and busy. After the changes it's a white background with only what is necessary for people to navigate the pages.

Another thing began happening after the changes too. More people began staying in the chat room for longer periods and we began getting more people listening. Why? How could something so simple make such a big difference?

Energy! It's all about the energy. We all feel it. We may not understand it but we react or respond to it anyway. The frequency of the website did not lift up or enhance the energy of the radio shows. So people would come to the website, see the chat, feel agitated and leave. Now they really wanted the message, just not the conflicting energy of the whole experience.

As a station owner I'm not concerned so much about how many are listening as I am to how long they listen. The length of their

connection with us shows me how the energy is flowing and how it's being received. When I noticed that people were listening out in cyber radio land longer than staying in the chat I put two and two together. Something about the energy of the website was the reason.

Again, it's energy, always about the energy. Perhaps you've taken the classes and read the books on selling. You've put BIG font all over your Splash Page. You have a pop up that requires people to give you their email address before they can get the FREE GIFT. What is the energy of that? Feel it. How does it feel. If I tell you I have something free for you but that in order to get it you have to give me something.. how free is the gift? Is it even a gift? No, it's a requirement.

The energy of free and having to give something, even an email address contradict each other. They don't cancel each other out, instead they create a little cyclone of chaos energy that people feel and run like the wind for.. or they come only for the free & you never hear from them again. This is the energy of this type of selling. It creates the opposite energy that you are offering.
If you are using this type of marketing to sale survivor supplies then it will work great. Let's talk about this for a minute. The hurry hurry sky is falling type of selling works great when you match it to the product with same energy. That's why people who are selling end of the world products use it. They realize that their market is in the Fight or Flight energy already. They use that to their advantage.

The energy is panic and fear. When you sale products that compliment panic and fear with the panic and fear energy you make loads of sales and money. It's easy when the energy works together. If I use these methods to sale a book on healing the

inner child or how to meditate for well being I would probably not get many sales. The reason is again simple.

The energy wave I'm broadcasting on brings the people who are tuned into that frequency. It's like the old radios where you had to turn a dial to connect with the signal. At any given moment there are probably millions of radio and TV signals going out. You don't hear or see them all, you only see or hear the ones you are tuned into.

So let's look at this further. If you are offering a book on healing your painful emotions or a class on meditating for physical health where do you think the people who are already ready and open to your book or class are tuned into? They are tuned into the wavelength, the energy of what they are ready for. If you broadcast your FM Frequency book or class on an AM or Ham Radio station the FM Frequency people are NOT there. You can't connect with them because they are not tuned into the energy you are broadcasting with.

A bit more about the HAM Radio before we move on. There is nothing wrong with being on this frequency. We are all at different places of experiencing ourselves. It's all good and perfect. My reason for breaking it down this way is to explain in plain words how this method of Sharing works when you are really sharing and not selling.

Selling is great for products that are intended for the people ready for them. It just doesn't work for those of us who are sharing healing, self awareness and consciousness. What we are digging into in this book is the Path of Sharing. It's a whole new energy. A new way to let the information flow easily like a fountain with sweet running water.

Selling works great for some things. For those of us sharing wisdom it's self defeating. We are now learning to connect with a new level of sharing ourselves and our messages so that those who are asking for them always connect with us. Easy Breezy is the way.

Chapter Two
AM Frequency

There is another frequency that is sold as a sure fire winner to spiritual authors, speakers, teachers and coaches. It's the AM Frequency. It's a delightful bandwidth where elementary school level products and services are offered to the public at large. There is nothing wrong with creating products and services offered on this frequency. There are many, many people who are here in their experience and spiritual understanding of themselves and their world.

It just doesn't work for everyone or every product. There is a reason for this. If you are offering products or services that relate to this energy it's a win win for you and your clients. This is generally the area where what I refer to as the "Law of Attraction Religion" people hang out. Nothing wrong with that either.. it's just another experience.

What I call the Law of Attraction Religion are those people who are still looking outside themselves for their answers. They still hold onto beliefs that there is something or someone out there who will fix everything for them. This is why the Law of Attraction books etc sale so well. They are based on the energy of out there somewhere, becoming or attracting so that you can have what you want.

I also refer to this as "Intellectual Spirituality". People here are still in the gather in the knowledge phase of life and experience. They buy one book after another, take one course after another. They are caught up in the energy of emotions and seek one experience after another to keep that feel good energy flowing. Again, nothing wrong with this.

We were all here at one time in our journey. Many reading this book may still be in this part of the journey back to self understanding. It's a good place to be.

You've begun to realize the connection between thoughts and emotions. You are even seeing the relationship to what you think about with strong feeling showing up on a steady basis. You are starting to put things together and come up with some ideas about those beliefs you hold.

People in this frequency are perfect for coaching, classes and books on connecting the dots between stuff and beliefs.
If your book, product or service falls into this category, then you will be successful as long as you broadcast on the frequency and don't slip back into the Ham Radio bandwidth.

AM Frequency still holds onto a few beliefs that are based in fear and worry. Thoughts and feelings are often seen as the enemy rather than roadsigns for the next great AHA insight.

Remember the outer is still more of a reality than the inner self to people listening and tuning in to this energy stream. Make sure that you keep your energy on this level or higher at all times. You don't want to slip into the fear broadcast and create more confusion.

Selling here is straightforward. Just be honest about what you are offering. State what the principles are, how they will help people to know more. People here are into knowing, facts, lists, affirmations, statements, actions that can be done to get into the "feel good groove". Nothing dishonest about offering these products and services.. just be plain about what you are sharing.

The AM Frequency is a powerful tool for getting your ideas and steps to something better to the world. As long as you don't clutter up your offer with all the FREE GIFTS and such energy, you will do well. You understand this process of getting into a better feeling emotional place. Things may not be totally the way you desire to experience them, but it's better. People do want this knowledge. They will use it to bring them into a better feeling life. From this place they will move onto the next level of FM Frequency.

While we are still in the AM broadcast zone let me remind you to share what you know. If you are writing a book, teaching, coaching or doing a radio show, stick with what you know right now. People can feel it when you are just repeating something you've read in a book or just listened to in a class. Sharing YOUR journey is key to success here. Actually, FM Frequency is all about Sharing YOUR journey.. what YOU Know with others.

AM Frequency folks want to know how to get more money, how to feel better in their emotions and body. They want steps to success. If you are an FM Frequency teacher don't sale here with this energy. Remember, you want to broadcast in the same frequency as that of your message. Don't try to share how to walk on water with people who are just looking for water.

Also if you don't know how to attract, create or manifest a million bucks don't offer information on how to do it. People will feel what you KNOW.. even if they don't realize what they are intuiting, they will still react or respond to the energy. Stick with what you know and you'll do great. Share from the place of your experience, your feelings, your understanding.

Regardless of whether you are an author, teacher, coach or radio host, being honest is always the purest energy to share on. While I'm in this area let me move a bit into coaching mode and offer information that will help you be clear about your own energy vibration.

Do you really KNOW what you are teaching? I'm asking this because over the years of coaching, teaching, doing radio shows etc., I've had many clients who have come to me and exclaim how now that they've worked with me they are ready to teach, coach etc. One young lady several years ago announced that she was going to be a parent coach. She had two very young children under the age of five.

I asked her if she was going to coach parents with children under the age of five? No, she said. She was going to coach all parents on how to be a good parent. I continued with a few more questions like, what will you tell the single parent of a rebellious 15 year old? Or what will you share with the dad of a grieving 10 year old who has just had his mother pass?

She didn't understand what I was getting at and moved ahead to establish herself as a parent coach. She's not doing that now. Smile

My point is this one. If you don't know it people will find out. They will find out quickly too. I only write books on things I have experienced. Not what I am experiencing, but what I've experienced. There is a difference in energy. If I only share what I'm doing right now there is not much to share. When I have walked through the knowledge and it's become wisdom and I move into the next expansion I have something to talk about.

As station owner I always tell the hosts who are having a problem with their broadcasts to focus only on what you KNOW. Let yourself be an open book, let the wisdom within you flow easily into the world. People feel that and connect with it. Don't try to act as though you have all the answers. When you put yourself on that pedestal something will always come along and take you down a few notches. You'll create the experience that will do it for you in due time.

I know a lot about a lot of things, but I've not even begun to know much. The more knowledge you gather the more knowledge you realize there is to learn.

That's why I encourage you to share Wisdom. Wisdom is your knowing.. your life, your path.

The AM Frequency is the perfect bandwidth for you to share how you got out of an awful job, or found your way out of depression. It's a perfect place to share your steps to making friends and feeling good. Stick with what you know. Share where you are and what brought you to this point.

Chapter Three
FM Frequency

Here we move into the deeper way of sharing. If you are here and I know you are or you wouldn't be reading this book, you are not playing in the fear or facts sandbox anymore. You are really into yourself. You experience bliss far more than anything else. You've begun the creating of your life the way you desire to experience yourself. You know who you are and that you are Divine Human.

Perhaps your book, coaching, or class is about the things you learned along the way to where you are know. You do have deep understanding of how what showed up in your life got there.. you did it! You are no longer in the blame shame game. You are taking responsibility for what you are experiencing knowing that you are the creator of your experiences.

This is the level of FM Frequency broadcasting. You know that you know. You are not tied to beliefs or a reactionary lifestyle, rather you are mindful, awake, aware, alert and involved consciously in what you are creating and experiencing. This is what people desire to know.

While everyone you share with may not be on this level, it's much easier to work to uplift than it is to downgrade your message so that others can understand. Whether you are writing a book, teaching a course, coaching or hosting a radio program, remember uplifting is half the effort of turning down your signal & message.

Let's say that you are sharing your journey through the dark places you've created and experienced. Now the Ham or AM frequencies would place your message in the energy of "poor me". I didn't do anything, it was done to me, see how people treat me, woe is me for my troubles is the energy here.

You've already walked there & it's not necessary for you to broadcast to people still there on the same wavelength that they are on. You desire to uplift people, to inspire and motivate them to live an empowered life. If you spend your time & energy focused on the woes you've encountered you are spinning your wheels in the mud, throwing it everywhere.

However, if you mention where you've walked through and what you understood that brought you to the next expression of yourself, then people understand. People do want your story. They want to know you are REAL.

Don't pretend that you've got it all figured out. People smell that and are turned off. Share where you've been always with the new understanding that came from the experience. Bring it around to how you realized that you were the creator, writer, director & actor in the play which was your life.

A big part of sharing on the FM Frequency is sticking with what you know, being honest, being real. How would you relate to a success coach who is flat broke, in foreclosure & doesn't have a pot to tinkle in? See what I mean? You may have come up with a great course, you may be in the middle of a major break through in your life.. but IF you Don't Know it.. don't share it.

It's just not honest, and people will quickly figure out that you are trying to sale them an FM idea that's really Ham radio. When you are honest about the message you have, where is the energy of it, and share it on that level or the higher level, people better relate to you and your message.

We all want to experience financial prosperity. We like paying our monthly expenses. It would be untrue to try to get people to think otherwise. Here is a BIG Tip... if your only reason for teaching, writing, hosting a radio show or other endeavor is money.. it will turn people off who are desiring to know more about how it all works.

It's all about energy, frequencies. When you understand that your words, actions, thoughts, books, courses, coaching.. all energy.. all a frequency of energy.. then you are on track to match the energy of your message with the energy of sharing it with the energy of the people you are sharing with.

It's a new mindset to match energy with energy. We've all been taught to sale, sale, sale. To promote ourselves over the top with freebies, special limited time offers. These do work to bring in people. The people these techniques bring to you are those still in the looking stage. They are not ready for your message. They wouldn't understand your message if you gave it to them free of charge. They are operating on the frequency of mind, emotion and reaction.

If this is the energy of your message then by all means use these methods to tell people about your product / service. BUT if your message is on the FM Band Frequency, these techniques will not be heard by those who desire your message. It's really simple. You always want to match your message, your book, coaching or radio broadcast to the energy of the people you are writing for, teaching or talking with.

I've covered the basic of how the different frequencies work and what is broadcast on them. I'm sure you understand the principles I'm discussing, after all you are reading this book.

You may be asking, "ok, Donna.. now what"?

Stay Tuned for the rest of the book.

Chapter Four
Getting the Message Out

Here is where it starts getting fun so hang on. You know you have a message right? You've walked through some tough spots, you realize that you are the creator of your experiences. You've even gone so far as to write these events and the messages, or lessons you've gotten down. Perhaps you've written a book, or now teach these principles of insight to others, maybe you coach people to aid them on their journey.

You might have done your fair share of webinars, splash pages, pop up email address grabbers and the like. You've tweeted and used Facebook and other social media to blast your opportunity to everyone you could find. Right?

As Dr. Phil says, "how's that working for ya"?

If you are pitching magic potions, fairy dust & get rich quick schemes with those techniques, it's probably working pretty good. People are showing up to grab your freebies and then high tail it to the next free offer. You can get people to show up with these techniques, for a while anyway. It's getting them to really connect with you that's the problem.

You have noticed that most people have either unsubscribed from your large email list or they just don't read the emails, if they ever did. You are looking for something that helps you to make connections that build on human / divine connections with those you are writing, teaching or coaching for.

The first few steps are easy. Let's start with some of the basics of changing how we share rather than sale. What is the power of words? How do they affect the energy of your message? Words are energy that when you speak them forth, you are setting a vibration energy into motion. Energy affects energy & is affected by energy. That's simple, but what does it mean and how does it pertain to your product or service?

Take a look at some of the popular and over used words to tell people what you are offering.

Special

Limited Time

Low Price

Transformation

Evolutionary

Awakening

Law of attraction

Attracting

Empowering

FREE FREE FREE

Free Call

Free Webinar

Free Video

Free Ebook

Free Mini book

One of a kind

You get the idea. How do all those words feel to you? What images and memories do they bring to your mind? Do you remember all those times years ago when you ran to and fro looking for all the free stuff hoping that your answers were there? You thought that maybe, just maybe someone was giving away the keys to The Kingdom.. showing you how to instantly get rich, find the love of your life or be two sizes smaller without having to do anything but feel good about it.

This is the mindset of people who react to this type of promotion. Now.. IF your product or service is on this level by all means continue doing it this way. You will feel great seeing all the people show up to listen to you and give you their email address. This is the mind/ego/emotion frequency. It's a great place to be, we've all been there. We start here, some stay longer than others.. but it's OK. It's also great to market to these folks. They are tilled up earth and you can sow many seed here. Keep your message in line with how they relate though.

I want to add here that using these words and these offers can be helpful for search engines and website meta tags. I'm not saying to never use them, I'm suggesting that your use of them not be the main energy you are setting forth.

Think of it this way. If someone came up with a great idea and told you in a language you don't speak, how much good would it do you? None. That's the point I'm making here. Share on a level that the people you are working with can actually understand and want to hear. I've spent years hosting radio shows & coaching. I've come to know that keeping my message in line with what people are actually asking is key to being heard and understood.

You wouldn't offer to sale college level math books to kindergarten students would you? Of course not.
Keep the transmission on the same level; what you are offering, how you are offering it and who you are offering it to. This is where the "sales pitch words" come into play.

If your desire is to give away as much free stuff as possible, to make quick one time only sales then the use of the "pitch words" is perfect. Social media is a good place to make these pitches too as most of the people who spend all day playing games and sending out quick cute remarks are lined up for this type of selling.

Keep your prices low, the pitch words cute & catchy & the email addresses will flow in. There is nothing wrong with this type of products or services. That's why I encourage you to continue with it if this is what you are offering to the public. Just remember to use the same frequency to promote as your product or service.

Now let's move on to how to use words for a different level of broadcasting. We've got our list of "hot" words that everyone uses over and over. You understand the "reaction" most people have to these words. This reaction is great if you are selling reaction products to reaction people.

But.. what if you are selling to people who have already figured out that for the most part these products and services are big promises that offer little substance. I'm not saying that your product is like that, but pointing out that most are. Why would you use words / energy connected to hype products if you are not selling hype products?

We all feel energy. Now we may not put it into words, but we are affected by the energy nonetheless. When you walk into a room and feel anger, you don't have to have witnessed the argument that took place moments before you got there. You FEEL it.

When your promotions are filled with hype, big promises, one of a kind, limited deals.. people are reminded of all the times before that they've taken the bait and how disappointed they were. Do you want them to feel and react that way to your promotions? NO, you don't.

So let's dig into the energy of words and how we react to them. Words are associated to our feelings which are connected to our experiences. If I start talking about going to the fair, you are reminded of when you went, how it smelled, sounded and whether or not you had a good time.

If I talk about holidays you begin remembering experiences around holidays, your emotions come into play. These Key Words & Phrases are used on purpose to cause an emotional reaction. You don't want to create an emotional reaction unless you are selling to reactionary people.

Reactionary people buy products that work on them emotionally. It's fine and good if this is where you are helping people. Feeling good or at least better about yourself is a big step in the awakening process, it's not the whole process though. If you are looking for deeper understanding you don't want hype. Keep this in mind. It's about energy, frequencies.

You have a journey to share. You are wiser than you were before you wrote the book or created the class or decided to coach. Perhaps you desire to go on air with your own radio program to share your story. This story is what people want to hear. They want to know about it. Not in a pity party kinda way either. They want you to take them with you on the journey, help them to see and feel your ups, downs and ups again.

The people you are offering wisdom to have already taken the path of get it quick, easy, magic, transformation, instant, I've got your answers way. They don't connect with this. In fact most often they don't give it a moments notice if they even see or hear about it.

More about the words and using them. Ask yourself what is your message. Write it down. What do you know? What are you sharing? How will it help others? How did it help you?
Until you can share your success story, not just a poor me I'm a victim story, you don't really have an FM Frequency message. Plain and simple, but true.
At this point of the book perhaps you'll see yourself as you really are believing yourself to be and make great progress on deeper understanding.

I've met many teachers, healers and speakers who are trying to teach on healing and success who are not there themselves and can't sell water to a dying man in the desert. How is that possible? It's energy. People know it even if they don't know the words, they feel the energy of it.

Over the years I've taught and coached many people who can not get clients because they are not being honest with themselves. I can't teach you something I don't know and you can't teach others what you don't know. Would you pay for healing from a healer who is always sick? No, you would not and neither will others.

Would you pay for success coaching from someone who is flat out penniless and being foreclosed on? I would hope not.

You have a success story don't you? Or do you just have an esoteric idea that you have not experienced? Here is a BIG KEY to connecting with people. People do want information.. but not just Intellectual Spirituality. This is what I refer to as those who have read all the self help books and have memorized all the key spiritual phrases. You know these people. You move away from them. You realize they are NOT living what they are teaching.

The new frequency is about Your Life. It's about YOU.

Chapter Five
Sharing YOU

We've covered a lot of information already. I've helped you build a foundation for what we are really talking about here. You understand the key words and phrases and the emotional reactionary method. You do not want to do this. You understand how what you have to share will not be heard on the other frequencies of sharing.

You have also determined what your success story is. Now let's talk about how to share it. There's a song that says, "want some human touch". I don't remember the rest of it, but that part is perfect for what people are looking for. They want real people with real experiences & real wisdom.

People want Experiential Spirituality!!!

As a teacher, coach & radio host I've seen my fair share of "teachers" who hear a few minutes of something and run off to create a new course or a seminar on that hours worth of information. Let me ask you, how much does someone really know when they take a few minutes of someone's information and teach it as their own wisdom? Not much.. and it shows.

Over the years I've had people work with me a few months & run off to start teaching or coaching what took me forty years to know & what they've invested a few hours in. Do you want to guess if they are being successful in it or not? Only those who run through clients like water through a sieve, and then only for a short time. This is selling and it's a lot of continuous work.

If you sale you must constantly be refilling your client base. When you share people tend to stay with you for long periods of time because you are reaching them on a soul level, not the mind or ego level. Mind and ego are always running about looking for the quick fix. The magic dust quest that will instantly create the life wanted with little or no personal responsibility on the part of the dreamer is all part of the Sales Mentality.

A few years ago I even wrote a book on this. " Pipe Dreamer or Conscious Creator" , still available at Amazon as a Kindle book. Selling is all about quick fix, big promises & emotional reaction. This type of selling reminds me of the old used car salesmen of the past, maybe they even still do it that way. It's pushy, desperate and not very pretty. Not only is it not pretty but it's just not working so great any longer. People are waking up to energy; to how things feel and whether or not it feels connecting and "right".

This mindset is just like any other program you create with. It's downloaded and doesn't require much thought on your part. As a radio station owner one of the biggest hurdles with new hosts who have done webinars is to change this mindset. It's obvious which hosts have been programed this way too. You will hear them say things on the air like; on this call, free gift, email address, newsletter, special offer, trial offer etc.

The energy around a webinar is to give someone a peek, just enough to hook them in and then deliver a sales pitch that hammers it home at the end. This type of selling isn't working very well for people I talk with on a regular basis. They host one webinar after another, spending untold hours networking, emailing, writing a new free something to give away, investing many hours and a lot of energy to get a very small financial return.

Let's look at the energy of this type of selling. First you are bringing in loads of Free Thought. What can I give away? How can I offer something exciting enough for free that people will show up for the free stuff and then maybe like what I say enough to work with me, is the energy you have set into motion. If you are setting the energy of what I call Free Free Free Gimme Gimme Gimme into motion you are already only broadcasting to people who are caught up in that energy.

You have a powerful book, course or coaching method. You know it worked because it's what you used to change your life. It's high level energy. There are many high level energy people out there just waiting for it too. They don't hear about it because you are broadcasting on a frequency that they are not listening on. You are broadcasting on the Free Gimme stations where only those who play with that energy hang out. They don't understand your message, it makes no sense to them. They are not in a place of personal experience & understanding that allows them to connect with your message.

Those that would "get it" don't hear about it because they are not hanging out on the Free Gimme Station Frequencies. That's the crux of the matter. The main point of the new way of Sharing to Sell is that example. You can't connect with people who are not in the same space as you are. If you are only using the old style methods of webinar or hard sale tactics to get your message out chances are very good that you are not making much progress.

I work with many people, mostly women, who have beautiful books, awesome coaching abilities and empowering messages who are so caught up in the sales pitch type of marketing that they just can't seem to sale anything anymore. You know what I'm talking about. You spend more time trying to find new clients and customers than you do actually working with clients and customers. There is a very good reason for this. The old style methods just don't work very well anymore and honestly before long they will not work at all in the area of spirituality and self help.

I'll give you an example. Recently I was having a conversation with a speaker telling about her coaching services. She was doing great in the beginning sharing her story & insights. When she got around to the part of talking about money, wealth & success she wasn't aware that her energy changed. From her body language to the pitch of her voice. After the meeting was over the gentleman in charge of the event spoke with her and said that it was obvious that she didn't KNOW the part about money & personal success. He asked her to learn that part of her message and come back to the event again when she had.
Not only was she offering an old fashioned Sales Pitch.. but it was obvious to those listening that she didn't KNOW her message. These two things are the main reasons people don't succeed in the "spiritual community". You may have a great idea, a wonderful personal story to share, but IF you don't know all your message, people will feel it.

Teach what you know. Period. If you are in the process of learning it then share the process on a radio show or in your blog, but don't try to package and sale it. People want answers, conclusions. If I stopped writing this book right now how would you feel about me as an author, this book, and the investment you made in the book? You'd feel that the part you really wanted to know was missing.. because it would be.

This is my main point with this book. Don't push cliff hangers on people. You know what I mean, remember when at the end of the season of your favorite series on TV when they left a BIG unanswered question at the end of the last minute. That type of promotion works to make sure you tune in the next season to find out what happens but when it comes to sharing wisdom, information about changing one's life, it will not wash. Make sure your message brings up the process to the problems, the process of figuring it out and ways to resolve them. Also be sure that the solution is a principle people can repeat without having to purchase your next book.

Honesty, integrity and being real is how you get your message out today. There are millions of people who are asking for what you are offering. By making sure that you are setting the energy of your message into motion on a level or frequency where your askers are, you make success for you and others a surety.

Another example for you. I heard a teacher on the air talking about spiritual principles for healing your life. When a question was asked directly to her she answered by saying that was in her program that you could buy on her website. The person who had asked the question made a snippy comment and left the chat room. What a wonderful opportunity this teacher had to share a bit of her process right then and there and afterwords give out her website address for those who wanted to work with her. She was trying so hard to "SALE" that she lost a client.

Yet another example will serve here for my next point. Recently I heard a radio host talking about anger & the problems around it. Someone in the chat asked for a meditation or something to help work through anger issues. The host promptly stated that was part of her step system & was available on her website to those who worked with her!!! Wow.. the chatters were shocked. Honestly I just smiled. This is part of the old system which is based in lack, fear, anxiety & don't give anything of value away or you will not have any business.

I'm not suggesting that you give away your books, or do coaching for free. I'm not even suggesting that you share all your "secrets" for free on the air. What I am stating is that you visit the reasons behind your way of sharing. Is it really sharing or fear based, lower vibration selling?

Years ago I realized that when I give away my wisdom on my radio broadcasts it actually helps my sales. Each week I host a show on two of my print books. Over the years I've read the whole books on the air and talked about them. I open to a new section each week, read a little bit and then expand on those principles. Has it kept people from buying my books? Nope. Actually as I expanded recently on how I built Awakened Radio on the principles in my book, "How To Thrive In A Survival Mindset World" the guy I was talking with on the phone interrupted me to ask where he could purchase a copy. Sale made without any selling at all on my part.

One of my personal mottoes is "give them something to take home in their pocket". I'm not talking about brochures or trinkets or freebies here. What I mean is always give real, helpful information to those you are sharing with. Don't pitch products up in the air to see if someone catches them. We are not cooking noodles throwing them against the wall to see if they stick so we'll know if they are done. When you are focused on using freebies to get people to show up or trial offers or introduction classes to build your relationships with people, realize that this is not a relationship. It's a freebie. Mostly only the Freebie Folks show up for this.

When I promote my coaching for example, I focus on how my work will help people in the areas I know I know what I'm talking about. What I've learned, where I've traveled are also included. I want people to get to know me. It's not about the paper work I have, but who I am, who I know myself to Be. Then I make the offer that working with me will provide guidance in the areas I'm good at. I don't offer coaching in areas where I am still working through my "stuff". People desire to know you. To connect with you. It's about the energy.

When you give the message that you are real, honest, live in integrity, that you share wisdom, not knowledge.. people get you. I don't write books on building machines or how electricity work simply because I have only a little knowledge on those topics. I have very little wisdom at all there. I DO have Wisdom in dealing with anger, with healing childhood issues, with parenting, with hosting a radio show, running a station etc. Those are the things I share. What I KNOW is what I offer to others.

It's not just about that Intellectual Spirituality either. People pick up pretty quickly if you are just quoting what you heard or read from someone else. I get tickled when I share with someone for an hour or so on a coaching call and the next thing I find they've just written a blog about it. It's actually a compliment while at the same time it makes the point that we are really caught up in intellectual knowing rather than wisdom. Wisdom is all about life experience. Knowledge is facts, figures, data. You can quote that back like reading a book. You can't go much further because it's not yours. It's not part of your experience.

Years ago I had a best friend who was in her fifties while I was in my mid twenties. She explained it this way. Intellect is your ability to gather information. It's the speed and ease with which you bring in facts & figures. Knowledge is the information gathered. Smart is being able to quote it back to someone. Wisdom is when you actually use the information to change your life. Wisdom is what we desire.

Wisdom is what we all yearn for, a working out in our lives of the information we've gathered is our goal. When sharing your product, book or service stay aware that this is really the main reason people are working with you or buying your book. They are not interested in more knowledge, mere information. They've gathered loads of that already over the years.

I explained it this way years ago. If knowledge were indeed "power" then all the books in all the world's libraries would be busily creating what was contained in their pages. Now we know that just the information isn't what changes things. People are figuring this out in waves of insight. We all want CHANGE. We want real change. We are not interested in more thoughts, more ideas, more theories. People want their lives to really really really BE different.

We've all gone through the stages of information gathering. How many books and classes have you bought over the years? Where is that information now? Are your book shelves lined with books that have awesome thoughts and ideas in them? The real question is how many of those ideas have you actually incorporated into your life so that you have really changed you?

This is what people want you to share. How you actually changed. Ideas are fantastic, as are books. As a radio host and author, it's pretty obvious that I love words and communication. I am also very aware that just the words without any meaning of them, without real understanding doesn't bring about the instant insights that people are looking for. Too many spiritual teachers, authors and coaches are stuck in the abstract fluff n puff of stuff.

Chapter Six
No More Puff n Fluff

You've probably noticed by now that I've broken this book down into small, bite size pieces and backed up, moved sideways and even explained the same thing several different ways. I did that on purpose. The reason is this; we all filter what we hear, read, or see through our own experiences and beliefs. The more ways you can share your message the more likely people are to actually grasp it. I'm not suggesting that you just say the same thing over and over, but always be sure to tie your pieces together so that it's easier for people to really understand.

Another main point I really want to impress on you the reader is that people are open to real, true, empowering stories. Your real, true and empowering stories are then the most powerful means of sharing your message that you have. You've walk a long ways to get where you are. That book, or coaching or healing work is the result of what you have experienced, what you've worked through and come to the true understanding of. This is what people want to know. They are interested in How You Did It.

Knowing that you, the teacher, healer or speaker have actually lived what you are sharing connects you. We've spent decades in the fluff n puff esoteric teachings. They feel good, but there are not real answers in them. It's great to feel OK while you are meditating, but what about when the kids are screaming, the car will not start and you can't pay the bills? Is it enough to just feel good?

Since The Secret came out people have tried to "become like a magnet" so they can "attract" what they want. For most it hasn't worked because the beliefs or operating programs are not about experiencing abundance, good relationships etc. Many have become even more frustrated than before they started reading the book. It's one thing to get a great parking spot.. but those don't pay the bills or heal relationships.

We've entered into a new phase of our understanding, knowing somehow that there is more to it than just feeling good for a while. We are ready to create on purpose what we really desire to experience. I will not go deeply into the "new thought", listen in to my radio show for more on that, (smile) it's enough for now for you to accept that people want something more, something deeper than just a surface feeling good teaching and message.

We've been taught over the years to wear certain colors, to use certain key words and be flashy on our websites to attract clients and make money. Emotional selling has been a big hit for many years, and honestly it still is for people living in the emotional addiction state. You are not writing, teaching, doing coaching or healing work for those people. There are still plenty of people emotionally addicted to feeling good and feeling good teachers. There are also many who have come forward from that and are actively looking for something with a bit more substance.

Chances are pretty good you were once one of the "emotionally addicted" people. You went from feel good teacher, books that promised the answers and followed up on every shiny thing that came on the market. Most of us have done that. Many have spent thousands of dollars on one after another class, program, coaching or Big Promise that felt great during the activity but then fell flat when it came time to go back to living your daily life.

These are the types of people I'm telling you how to market to. It's not even marketing. It's a way of letting people know who you are and how you know what you know that allows them to "know you", connect with you, that I'm sharing. Sharing is what it's all about. It's the FM Frequency.

Learning to trust yourself, to share your wisdom, to be real is the new way to work with people who are ready for your message.

Let's talk a bit more about puff n fluff teaching and selling. I've mentioned words before, actually, I talk a lot about words because they are energy. We often use words that we've picked up from others that feel catchy. Yes.. that's how they feel. They are fad words or catch phrases. Most of the time we don't even know what we are saying. The words just sound spiritual.

I'll go through a few of them for you.

Living from your heart

Your Authentic Self

Living in love

Staying centered

Being Balanced

In the vortex

In the flow

Now let's talk about emotional selling.. the Fluff n Puff Intellectual Spirituality Esoteric Mumbo Jumbo method.

Look again at the words and phrases above. Just exactly what do these phrases mean? I'm not saying there is anything "wrong" with the words or phrases. I am pointing out that quite often we grab onto cute phrases and uses them over and over without any meaning and people feel that. With all the build up to how awesome 2012 was going to be, the one thing that did happen, is people are more open to energy. They are more understanding of your energy. The hype of 2012 is a good example of what I'm sharing here. The world was ready for a TRANSFORMATION to instantly take place. People were promising that BLISS was a second away.. something was going to happen to change them in an instant and it didn't happen.

It's understandable that people are a bit more aware of what is being said, and the energy of what is spoken. Even before you open your mouth to speak your "energy signature" has already informed everyone around you of who you are. Understand that not only are people feeling the "real eternal" you, but all the masks, the games, the persona that you are bringing with you are felt as well. If you are not being honest about who you are, what you know.. people feel it and either react or respond.

This type of selling is based on emotional needs. It works too. People have used it for years and still do. Many make big bucks working up people's emotions to get them to react with a purchase. If your product or service is for emotional pleasure only, then continue with this method.

A few good examples of what I'm talking about are the hype of The Secret and 2012. People got all worked up like they were at a tent revival. Something was promised to happen. They felt good, they were excited. They bought to books, took the courses, took the cruises. They lined up in groves to be changed.

Then... blam.. nothing much happened. No changes occurred. Why? Simply because EMOTION ONLY does NOT change you or your life! The majority of clients I've worked with in the past five years did all the "secret" stuff.. the "vortex" stuff.. and when they got to me their question was, "Ok, now how do I DO THIS"? People want to know HOW.

You are the teacher of the HOW. This is your message. You don't have to use gimmicks and tricks, you don't have to create an energy of urgency or lack to get people to buy your book, listen to your radio broadcast or take your course. You have answers. Real Answers. This is what people want.

Let's talk a minute about reaction and responding. Reacting is when you are in emotions. You aren't really thinking about anything, you are in auto mode. Something happens that is sort of like something that's already happened and you just instantly act the same way you did the other times. This is emotion and ego working.

This is the old energy of selling. You know it when you feel it and so do your clients, listeners. This type of selling or promoting is based on very low energy vibrations of fear and not enough. You feel desperate and in a desperate energy rush you push buttons to get people to react. I could name a few famous people who still it this way. They make loads of money at it too. It works if you are selling emotional based, fear based products and services to emotional and fear based people.

Let me share a true story. Over 20 years ago I was selling security systems by setting up appointments over the phone. The guideline for getting people to say yes to us on the phone was to frighten people. We were supposed to remind people of how much crime had taken place in just the last month or so in their area. The other people in the office were using this means of pre-selling the security systems, but I refused. I would not go along with selling based on fear. There was a need in some areas for the system and I pre-sold based on facts without the fear energy.

The guy in charge of the office got very upset with me because I would not follow his instructions. He informed me that the owner was coming to the office and wanted to speak with me. When the owner called me into the office he wanted to know why I refused to use the script and rules as I was told to. I informed him that I had no intention of frightening the elderly into buying something. I asked him how he would feel if I called his mother or grandmother and scared them half silly in order to sale his security system. He thought about it a few minutes and then stated that from now on the script would be changed and people should follow my lead as I was the number one sales person in the whole company.

Not only did I pre-sale the most, but I had the highest percentage of actual sales. People that actually had the systems installed. My sales were solid because they were NOT fear based. People didn't say yes to me on the phone because they were reacting. They said yes to me and when the installer showed up with the system and the paper work they were ready to sign on the dotted line. I had given out the information and allowed people to see the value in what I was selling.

This is FM Frequency. It works. It also empowers your clients. It gives them the message that you respect them. You are allowing a space for them to be responsible for their creations. When you work and live in this energy you are lifting yourself and others to a higher level of expression. You are saying to the world that what you teach is true, it works. You don't need gimmicks and tricks when your message is honest and uplifting.

All the hype about 2012 really helped a lot of people wake up to the What Now question. They realized that all the emotionally charged gimmicks didn't take them where they wanted to experience themselves. On Awakened Radio the hosts with the most success are the ones who are honest about their own journey. They teach what they KNOW. They are gimmick free messengers of wisdom. Wisdom is what Evolutionary Spirituality is all about.

I'll be honest with you. If you are selling emotional products to emotional people.. keep on with it. It's not about one product or style being better than another. What I'm sharing is the different types of products and how to match the energy of the product with the energy of the person wanting the product. If you are reading this book you've already done the free stuff, webinars, introduction offers, gathering emails, send out promotions weekly thing. You've worked yourself silly in an effort to let people know about the awesome new method of healing, creating, empowered living that you've discovered. You know your product is good. It worked for you and you just know if you can tell others about it that it will help them too.

The problem has been how to tell them. How do you get your message in front of the people it's created for? That the real issue I'm dealing with in this book. I've talked with women all around the world who are wondering the same thing. How can I get my product to the people I created it for? It's about the energy. That's the bottom line.

We've looked at a few types of products and styles of promoting them. By now you have a pretty good idea of where your product is. Remember, there is no good or bad here, just different types, different expressions. The energy of your product, your energy and the energy of your intended client just all need to line up. If you are broadcasting on a channel where emotionally based clients are with a FM message chances are you will not be heard or understood. You want to get YOUR message to the people who are willing, ready and happy to hear it. We've all done the process of writing down what our business goals are. Well, here we go again. Take a few minutes to make note of what your message really is. What are you saying? Why are you saying it? How are you saying it? These are all very important in marketing. Even though we are spiritual teachers, we are still marketing. We are finding ways to let people know about our books, courses, radio broadcasts etc. We all want to make money doing it too. I'm not giving away this book. I'm offering it for an energy exchange that we call money. I'm honest about that part. I, like you, have expenses, outflows of money energy in my life. We call them electricity, water, internet, food, transportation and clothing.

I strongly suggest that you be very honest about the money part of your message. Money is important. It's the way we've set things up to interact with all those conveniences and perks. I do a little dance of joy each time someone buys a book from me or takes a class. Being spiritual is being totally interactive in all aspects of life. Money is a part of that. Poverty is not the highest expression for spiritual teachers. We all know that, but experiencing it means we must do our own inner shadow work and come to terms with our beliefs and programs about money. Now you may be asking why I'm inserting this in the middle of a book on promoting your product. The answer is very important. Until we are OK with money our energy will not be a consistent FM Frequency. Emotions of lack, fear, worry will creep in to our promotion. Even if we stay away from all the obvious trick words and phrases, people will feel our relationship with money.

Remember, it's all about the energy in the now and beyond. 2012 got us ready for a new way of actually experiencing ourselves. Now it's time to live all that stuff we've gathered and stored in our intellect. Money is the key issue and reason people go back to the

tricks of old selling techniques. If you are not OK with money in YOUR life it will pop up over and over again. I'll give a few more examples here of what I'm talking about.

When How To Thrive In A Survival Mindset World was ready for sale I went to a group on Facebook that I was a member of. I was so excited to get this information out there to the world. I KNEW this was good stuff. I had lived the principles in that book. I had transformed my experience with the information before it even became a book. I was delighted, excited and ready to share it with everyone. So, I went to a spiritual based group to share the news that it was ready and where to get a copy. Facebook notified me that comments had been made to my post so I popped over there to see what people were saying. Several people shared my excitement and had great things to say. ONE person commented that I was a "prophet for profit". WOW! Bam! Imagine my surprise at that statement? Me? A prophet for profit? Was I reading that right? I sat there for a bit and pondered the message. Not the written words but the meaning they had for me. The meaning I gave the words. Did I really want to be a prophet for profit???
YES YES YES! I did want to profit from my sharing by sitting for many hours in front of my keyboard writing down my wisdom on how to Thrive. I really did expect to profit through the sharing of my wisdom. I'd taken more than fifty years to remember all that great stuff and months to write it all down and turn it into a book. Being a profiting prophet was exactly what I wanted to Be.

Coming to that conclusion took me through a process of being really honest with myself about how I felt about money and me in relationship to money. I remembered how aggravated I'd felt growing up in church hearing the preacher say that we should give our money to the church, that GOD needed it and expected it. There was still some stuff there, hidden deep inside my programming that was ready to come out and be let go of. I did

the shadow work. I was honest with myself about how that old feeling many years before had played out in my giving away without asking for money in return. I realized that my "belief program" about money was why it had been so hard for me to experience a steady flow of the stuff in my life. I went through all those old notions about hard work, money being dirty, spiritual people being poor if they were really spiritual.

I could have just gotten angry or felt offended and stayed in the same old belief / act / creation patterns. BUT I didn't. Neither should you. It's time for all of us prophets to make a profit. The notion that really spiritual people should not be very, very rich is chicken ca ca. It's time to put that on the compost pile and use it to grow our experience of abundance. I've run into a few "money teachers" who don't have two nickels to rub together. How can that be? It's easy. They know the intellectual aspects of being prosperous, but they haven't cleared out the belief programs that hinder their actual experience of prosperity. I want to inject something else here that is very, very important about your message and money. IF you are creating products for the sole purpose of making money, that's your only goal, to make money, you are not on FM Frequency. Furthermore people will know it, they will feel it. While I started this book to explain how to market without the hard sale, it's moved into a book that helps you actually get into the groove of what you are doing, why you are doing it and how to do it for the best results. Creating products JUST TO MAKE money has fear and lack at their base.

Let's talk a few minutes about this energy. A few years ago I began to notice that a lot of my coaching clients wanted to be a coach after a few sessions with me. I was a bit shocked at first. Now, don't get me wrong, I think being a life coach is a wonderful thing, that's why I do it. However, when you are still figuring out your own mess what do you really have to share? How can you teach what you don't know? These are the questions I asked a

few of the women. I also find this curious on other topics, people who teach how to get rich when they themselves don't have two nickels to rub together. What do you have to teach? I can't teach Greek simply because I don't know it. I could take lessons and begin teaching what I'm learning as I go, but honestly who would want to take classes from me?

This is what so many experience. You want to make money. You want to help others as a way to make money. That's all well and good. BUT!
This is the important part. If you are not sharing a message of wisdom, life experience that is growing, expanding, working in your own life, people feel it. If you have created a product just to make money because you are desperate for money, people feel it. My best advice is Share What You Know. Whether you are broadcasting a radio show or teaching, coaching or writing books.. Share What You Know.

It takes honesty to work through your own reasons for what you are doing. Yes, you want to help people. But do you have as a bigger reason the "need" for money? We all use money to get along in this world, but what I mean by "need" is deeper than that. It's based in a fear, a belief in lack. An energy about money that makes it hard to get, that I've just got to get it, that I don't have enough, I must work harder, do anything, everything or the world will end.. is FEAR. People feel it too. The FM Frequency is for those of us who have already worked through our worries and struggles with money. I'm not saying that you must be a billionaire to have worked through this. I am saying that you are understanding that MONEY is NOT the real issue. What you want is an experience. The experience of a big, nice home, new care, travel, etc. You understand that the experience is the desire.. the money is just a tool used in the experience. Say you want to go to the store. You don't sit around trying to manifest a store or the items in the store. You know the store already exists and that

it's fully stocked. The store is the experience you desire to have. Your car is the tool, the middle man to get you to the desired experience. You don't work hard to manifest a way to get to the store. You get in your car, call a taxi or take a bus and move towards the desired experience.

Money is like the car. It's the middle man, the tool, the vehicle for moving into the experience that already exists. Stop chasing after the middle man. Cease at once your struggle with money. Just stop it. Change your understanding of money and your relationship with it will change as your experiences just magically unfold slap dab in the middle of your life. As you make this change your business will change as well. Your energy really IS your business. When it's all lined up and meshing together without the conflicting beliefs and actions, magic happens. This is what you share. The magic. That's your true message. Share How You Do It. That is what people want to know. That's what people are willing to exchange money for. How To is where we are now. While the Awakening Process was all about facing our fears of things ending, greed, worry, and fear; Evolutionary Spirituality is all about releasing what doesn't work and starting where you are right now with a deep, working understanding of who you are and how things work.

Those of us in the "spiritual community" have spent years and loads of money to find the next secret to life. We've created conflict and confusion. Now it's time to just stop it. Drop the old beliefs and the old ways of doing things. Start where you are right now. To this point in the book you've been having a conversation with yourself. Take a few hours to write down that conversation. Make lots of notes. What have you read that you agreed with and what did you disagree with? After getting that down on paper take time to find out why you agree or disagree. What are the beliefs that have been confronted while reading this book? Do you feel that what I say is opposite your best coach or

friend's advice and you must lean their way? Personally, it doesn't matter to me whether you believe me, agree with me or not. Your reaction or reaction doesn't change what I KNOW. I'm not being a smart Alec either. My message is to share what I know. Those who are asking for what I know will hear me and do something with the wisdom I share. Those who don't want it just don't want it. It's OK with me. My message is sharing what I KNOW WORKS. It will not work for every single person where they are right now. If you haven't done your shadow work, taken out the garbage of outdated beliefs, chances are this book isn't working for you. It is planting seed though. Those seed over time will germinate and grow. That's why I ask to to take time to sort through how you feel about what I've written so far. Getting insight into where you are on this topic will aid you in moving forward into the next steps of sharing and being a prophet who actually profits.

Chapter Seven
Pulling it all Together

We've covered a lot of information since I first had the idea and began writing this little book. What began as a way to share how to better tell the world about your message has morphed into how to better know your message as you share your message. That always happens with me. I understand the process of this too. It's all written down in my book How To Thrive In A Survival Mindset World. The idea is the seed. Once planted the seed grows and produces many times more of itself than you started off with. This is how life works. You set an energy into motion and it expands. It creates more of itself, creating in it's own energy. No matter the energy set it motion, it always does this. This is Creative Energy in action.

The more aware you are of what you really desire, the more aware you of of the experience you wish to have, the less burdened you are by limiting beliefs, the easier and more magically you live your dreams and the more you have to share with others. Teaching what you KNOW is key. So, knowing must come before the teaching.

Bottom line is this. You are your brand. You are your business. Especially now people want real. They don't want pretty key phrases they've already heard. People are looking for teachers who do more than teach. People are looking for Way Showers, those who show the way by walking it. You are this kind of person or you wouldn't be reading this book. You've come a long way over the years. You've sorted through a lot of twisted beliefs that kept you experiencing the same old unwanted stuff. Now you are ready to share.

There are loads of books on the market telling you how to market. I'm not teaching marketing. That's the old way for old subjects. I'm teaching you how to share a message that is YOU. You are the message you have to tell others about. You aren't just selling a book, hosting a radio show or teaching a class about stuff. You are sharing your life wisdom with all who will listen. You are seeing the pieces all starting to fall into place. Reading through this book and writing your notes has brought up a lot of stuff for you. Some of it you are celebrating and some you might be tempted to push back down. Celebrate both. Let whatever has come up for you that feels uncomfortable reveal it's gifts of deeper understanding, and healing.

A few words to finish it all up. Live each day remembering that you are planting seed, always planting seed. Trust the Invisible to germinate these seed. Know that they will grow, bloom, and present you with a bountiful harvest. Be open to accepting. Be willing to receive. This is one of the easiest ways to stay out of the desperation feeling that shows up now and again. Even when things don't seem to be working the way you want them to, TRUST the process of Thrival Energy Principles. Know that Creator is Always answering you with a yes. Trust, be willing, receive, celebrate the lifestyle of success that you are co-creating with all the energy you are setting into motion.

Thank you!

I really do appreciate your reading my little book. I know that it has brought you as much insight as it has me. I know when a book is good by how much reading it through the editing process inspires and teaches me.

I'd love to hear from you, you feedback is always welcome. Please leave a review for the book and share the information with your friends.

To contact me send email to donnadevane@gmail.com

I am available for interviews and love being a guest.

For more information about me and what I love doing visit my websites.

Www.EvolutionarySpiritualityCoaching.com

www.TheBarefootGuru.com

To find out more about the Awakened Radio Network & Thrive Evolutionary Consciousness Magazine visit

Www.AwakenedRadio.net

You ARE your Message

I love you,
Love yourself well

Donna DeVane
The Barefoot Guru

www.ingramcontent.com/pod-product-compliance
Lightning Source LLC
Chambersburg PA
CBHW061518180526
45171CB00001B/234